D0119095

Italian Regional Cooking

STEP-BY-STEP

Italian Regional Cooking

ROSEMARY WADEY

SHOOTING STAR PRESS

This edition printed in 1995 for:
Shooting Star Press Inc
230 Fifth Avenue – Suite 1212
New York, NY 10001

Shooting Star Press books are available at special discounts for bulk purchases for sales promotions,
premiums, fund-raising, or educational use. Special edition or book excerpts can also be created to
specification. For details contact: Special Sales Director, Shooting Star Press Inc.,
230 Fifth Avenue, Suite 1212, New York, NY 10001

ISBN 1 56924 186 4

Printed in Italy

Acknowledgements:

Design & DTP: Pedro & Frances Prá-Lopez / Kingfisher Design
Art Direction: Clive Hayball
Managing Editor: Alexa Stace
Special Photography: Martin Brigdale
Home Economist: Jill Eggleton
Cover Photography: Clive Streeter
Step-by-Step Photography: Karl Adamson
Step-by-Step Home Economist: Joanna Craig
Stylist: Helen Trent

Photographs on pages 6, 22, 38, 48 & 62: By courtesy of ZEFA

Contents

✤

ANTIPASTO & SOUPS *page* 7

Fish Soup...8
Red Bean Soup..10
Minestrone with Pesto...................................13
Eggplant Salad...14
Mozzarella in Carroza....................................17
Crostini alla Fiorentina..................................18
Seafood Salad...21

PASTA & PIZZA *page* 23

Tortellini..24
Sicilian Spaghetti...27
Gnocchi Romana..29
Polenta...31
Tagliatelle with Pumpkin...............................32
Milanese Risotto..34
Calabrian Pizza..36

FISH & SHELLFISH *page* 39

Baked Sea Bass...40
Sardine & Potato Bake....................................42
Trout in Red Wine..44
Squid Casserole..46

MEAT & POULTRY *page* 49

Pizzaiola Steak...51
Vitello Tonnato..52
Pot Roast Leg of Lamb...................................54
Saltimbocca...56
Chicken with Green Olives.............................59
Liver with Wine Sauce...................................61

DESSERTS *page* 63

Tiramisu..64
Zabaglione...67
Panforte di Siena..68
Pear Tart..71
Caramelized Orange.......................................73
Ricotta Ice Cream..74

ITALIAN FOOD BY REGION *page* 76

The Italian Regions....................................76-9
Pasta Dough...76
Cooking Pasta...77
Main Pasta Varieties.......................................78

Index..80

CHAPTER ONE

Antipasto & Soups

❦

The word antipasto means "before the main course" and what is served may be simple and inexpensive or highly elaborate. Antipasto usually comes in three categories: meat, fish, and vegetables. There are many varieties of cold meats, including ham, invariably sliced paper-thin. The best known is prosciutto from Parma, but there are many others, especially from the mountain areas, all of which can be served with slices of melon and figs. Numerous vegetables feature in antipasto dishes, served raw or marinated, deep-fried or pickled, with and without dressings. All varieties of fish are combined for the *antipasto di pesce*, often depending on availability but including inkfish, octopus and cuttlefish. Huge shrimp and mussels appear in various guises and fresh sardines are always popular. Soups, too, are a very important part of the Italian cuisine. They vary in consistency from very thin to virtually knife and fork soups. Minestrone is known worldwide but the best-known version probably came from Milan; however, all varieties are full of vegetables, often with pasta or rice plus beans, and are delicious and satisfying. Fish soups abound in one guise or another, and most of these are village specialities, so the variety is unlimited. Many of these soups constitute a whole meal, particularly those with a large proportion of beans, or with lightly toasted slices of bread added to the bowl.

Opposite: *The Grand Canal, Venice. With its close proximity to the sea, fish and seafood dishes are found in abundance around Venice and the north-east corner of Italy.*

STEP 1a

STEP 1b

STEP 4

STEP 5

FISH SOUP

All over Italy the selection of fish is enormous. There are many varieties of fish soup, some including shellfish. You will find cream soups, thin soups and thick soups: this one, from Tuscany, is more like a chowder.

SERVES 4-6

2 lb assorted prepared fish (including mixed
   fish fillets, squid, etc.)
2 onions, peeled and thinly sliced
a few sprigs of parsley
2 bay leaves
2 celery sticks, thinly sliced
$^2/_3$ cup white wine
4 cups water
2 tbsp olive oil
1 garlic clove, crushed
1 carrot, peeled and finely chopped
1 x 15-oz can peeled tomatoes, puréed
2 potatoes, peeled and chopped
1 tbsp tomato paste
1 tsp freshly chopped oregano or $^1/_2$ tsp
   dried oregano
$2^1/_2$ cups fresh mussels
1 cup peeled shrimp
2 tbsp freshly chopped parsley
salt and pepper
crusty bread, to serve

1 Cut the cleaned and prepared fish into slices or cubes and put into a large saucepan with 1 sliced onion, the parsley sprigs and bay leaves, 1 sliced celery stick, the wine, and the water. Bring to the boil, cover, and simmer for about 25 minutes.

2 Strain the fish stock and discard the vegetables. Skin the fish, remove any bones and reserve.

3 Heat the oil in a saucepan, finely chop the remaining onion and fry with the garlic, remaining celery, and carrot until soft but not colored. Add the puréed canned tomatoes, potatoes, tomato paste, oregano, reserved stock and seasonings. Bring to the boil and simmer for about 15 minutes or until the potato is almost tender.

4 Meanwhile, thoroughly scrub the mussels. Add to the saucepan with the shrimp and simmer for about 5 minutes or until the mussels have opened (discard any that stay closed).

5 Return the fish to the soup with the chopped parsley, bring back to the boil and simmer for 5 minutes. Adjust the seasoning.

6 Serve the soup in warmed bowls with chunks of fresh crusty bread, or put a toasted slice of crusty bread in the bottom of each bowl before adding the soup. If possible, remove a few half shells from the mussels before serving.

STEP 1

STEP 2

STEP 4

STEP 5

RED BEAN SOUP

*Beans feature widely in Italian soups, making them hearty and tasty.
You can use other varieties of beans in this soup
(from Tuscany and Lazio), if preferred.*

SERVES 4-6

*scant 1 cup dried red kidney beans, soaked
    overnight*
7¹/₂ cups water
1 large ham bone or bacon knuckle
2 carrots, peeled and chopped
1 large onion, peeled and chopped
2 celery sticks, thinly sliced
1 leek, trimmed, washed and sliced
1-2 bay leaves
2 tbsp olive oil
2-3 tomatoes, peeled and chopped
1 garlic clove, crushed
1 tbsp tomato paste
tbsp arborio or Italian rice
1¹/₄-1¹/₂ cups green cabbage, finely shredded
salt and pepper

1 Drain the beans and put into a
saucepan with enough water to
cover. Bring to the boil and boil hard for
15 minutes, then reduce the heat and
simmer for 45 minutes. The hard boiling
is essential to remove the toxins from the
red beans. Drain.

2 Put the beans into a clean
saucepan with the measured
amount of water, ham bone or knuckle,
carrots, onion, celery, leek, bay leaves,
and olive oil. Bring to the boil, cover and
simmer for an hour or until the beans are
very tender.

3 Discard the bay leaves and bone,
reserving any ham pieces from the
bone. Remove a small cupful of the beans
and reserve. Purée or liquidize the soup
in a food processor or blender and return
to a clean saucepan.

4 Add the tomatoes, garlic, tomato
paste, rice, and plenty of seasoning,
bring back to the boil and simmer for
about 15 minutes or until the rice is
tender.

5 Add the cabbage and reserved
beans, and ham and continue to
simmer for 5 minutes. Adjust the
seasoning and serve very hot. If liked, a
piece of toasted crusty bread may be put
in the base of each soup bowl before
ladling in the soup. If the soup is too
thick, add a little boiling water or stock.

MINESTRONE WITH PESTO

One of the many versions of minestrone, which is always full of a variety of vegetables, pasta and rice and often includes beans. This soup is flavored with pesto sauce, so often added to pasta dishes.

STEP 1

SERVES 6

scant 1 cup dried cannellini or other white beans, soaked overnight
10 cups water or stock
1 large onion, peeled and chopped
1 leek, trimmed and thinly sliced
2 celery stalks, very thinly sliced
2 carrots, peeled and chopped
3 tbsp olive oil
2 tomatoes, peeled and roughly chopped
1 zucchini, trimmed and thinly sliced
2 potatoes, peeled and diced
1 cup elbow macaroni (or other small macaroni)
salt and pepper
4-6 tbsp Parmesan, grated

PESTO:

2 tbsp pine nuts
5 tbsp olive oil
2 bunches fresh basil, stems removed
4-6 garlic cloves, crushed
3/4 cup pecorino or Parmesan, grated
salt and pepper

1 Drain the beans, rinse, and place in a saucepan with the measured water or stock. Bring to the boil, cover and simmer gently for 1 hour.

2 Add the onion, leek, celery, carrots, and oil. Cover and simmer for 4-5 minutes.

3 Add the tomatoes, zucchini, potatoes and macaroni, and seasoning, cover again and continue to simmer for about 30 minutes or until very tender.

4 Meanwhile, make the pesto. Fry the pine nuts in 1 tablespoon of the oil until pale brown, then drain. Put the basil into a food processor or blender with the nuts and garlic. Process until well chopped. Gradually add the oil until smooth. Turn into a bowl, add the cheese and seasoning and mix thoroughly.

5 Stir 1½ tablespoons of the pesto into the soup until well blended, simmer for a further 5 minutes and adjust the seasoning. Serve very hot, sprinkled with the cheese.

STEP 2

STEP 3

PESTO

Store in an airtight container for up to a week in the refrigerator; or freeze (without adding the cheese) for several months.

STEP 5

STEP 2

STEP 3

STEP 4

STEP 5

EGGPLANT SALAD

A first course with a difference from Sicily. It has a real bite, both from the sweet-sour sauce, with its surprising flavoring of chocolate, and from the texture of the celery.

SERVES 4

2 large eggplant, about 2 lb
salt
6 tbsp olive oil
1 small onion, peeled and finely chopped
2 garlic cloves, crushed
6-8 celery sticks
2 tbsp capers
12-16 green olives, pitted and sliced
2 tbsp pine nuts
1 square bittersweet chocolate, grated
4 tbsp wine vinegar
1 tbsp brown sugar
salt and pepper
2 hard-boiled eggs, sliced, to serve
celery leaves or curly endive, to garnish

1 Cut the eggplant into 1-in cubes and sprinkle liberally with 2-3 tablespoons salt. Leave to stand for an hour, to extract the bitter juices, then rinse off the salt thoroughly under cold water, drain and dry on paper towels.

2 Heat most of the oil in a skillet and fry the eggplant cubes until golden brown all over. Drain on paper towels, then transfer them to a large bowl.

3 Add the onion and garlic to the skillet with the remaining oil and fry very gently until just soft. Cut the celery into ½-in slices, add to the pan and fry for a few minutes, stirring frequently, until lightly colored but still crisp.

4 Add the celery to the eggplant with the capers, olives, and pine nuts and mix lightly.

5 Add the chocolate and vinegar to the residue in the skillet with the sugar. Heat gently until melted, then bring up to the boil. Season with a little salt and plenty of freshly ground black pepper, and pour over the salad. Mix lightly, cover, leave until cold, and then chill thoroughly.

6 Serve with sliced hard-boiled eggs and garnish with celery leaves or curly endive.

NOTE

This salad will keep for several days in a covered container in the refrigerator. Chopped green tomatoes may also be added to this salad, in season.

MOZZARELLA IN CAROZZA

A delicious way of serving cheese, a specialty of Campania and the Abruzzi. The cheese stretches out into melted strings as you cut it to eat. Some versions have prosciutto added, too.

SERVES 4

7 oz mozzarella
4 slices, about 3 oz, prosciutto
8 slices white bread, preferably 2 days old, crusts removed
a little butter for spreading
2 - 3 eggs
3 tbsp milk
vegetable oil, for deep frying
salt and pepper

TOMATO AND PEPPER SAUCE:
1 onion, peeled and chopped
2 garlic cloves, crushed
3 tbsp olive oil
1 red bell pepper, cored, seeded and chopped
1 x 15-oz can peeled tomatoes
2 tbsp tomato paste
3 tbsp water
1 tbsp lemon juice
flat-leaf parsley, to garnish (optional)

1 First make the sauce: fry the onion and garlic in the oil until soft. Add the bell pepper and continue to cook for a few minutes. Add the tomatoes, tomato paste, water, lemon juice and seasoning, bring up to the boil, cover and simmer for 10-15 minutes or until tender. Cool the sauce a little, then purée or liquidize until smooth and return to a clean pan.

2 Cut the mozzarella into 4 slices so they are as large as possible; if a square piece of cheese cut into 8 slices. Trim the ham slices to the same size as the cheese.

3 Lightly butter the bread and use the cheese and ham to make 4 sandwiches, pressing the edges well together. If liked, they may be cut in half at this stage. Chill.

4 Lightly beat the eggs with the milk and seasoning in a shallow dish.

5 Carefully dip the sandwiches in the egg mixture until well coated; if possible leave to soak for a few minutes.

6 Heat the oil in a large saucepan or deep-frier until it just begins to smoke, or until a cube of bread browns in about 30 seconds. Fry the sandwiches in batches until golden brown on both sides. Drain well on crumpled paper towels and keep warm. Serve the sandwiches hot, with the reheated tomato and pepper sauce, and garnished with parsley.

STEP 1

STEP 2

STEP 3

STEP 6

CROSTINI ALLA FIORENTINA

A coarse pâté from Tuscany that can be served as a first course or simply spread on small pieces of crusty fried bread (crostini) to serve as an appetizer with drinks.

SERVES 4

3 tbsp olive oil
1 onion, peeled and chopped
1 celery stick, chopped
1 carrot, peeled and chopped
1-2 garlic cloves, crushed
3/4 cup chicken livers
4 oz calf's, lamb's or pig's liver
2/3 cup red wine
1 tbsp tomato paste
2 tbsp freshly chopped parsley
3-4 canned anchovy fillets, finely chopped
2 tbsp stock or water
2-3 tbsp butter
1 tbsp capers
salt and pepper
small pieces of fried crusty bread (see right)
chopped parsley, to garnish

1 Heat the oil in a saucepan, add the onion, celery, carrot, and garlic, and cook gently for 4-5 minutes or until the onion is soft, but not colored.

2 Meanwhile, rinse and dry the chicken livers. Dry the calf's or other liver, and slice into strips. Add the liver to the saucepan and fry gently for a few minutes until the strips are well sealed on all sides.

3 Add half the wine and cook until mostly evaporated, then add the rest of the wine, tomato paste, half the parsley, anchovy fillets, stock or water, a little salt and plenty of black pepper.

4 Cover the pot and simmer for 15-20 minutes or until tender and most of the liquid has been absorbed.

5 Cool the mixture a little, then either coarsely chop or put into a food processor and process until coarsely blended.

6 Return to the saucepan and add the butter, remaining parsley and capers, and heat through gently until the butter melts. Adjust the seasoning and turn into a bowl. Serve warm or cold spread on the slices of crusty bread and sprinkled with chopped parsley.

CROSTINI

To make crostini, slice a crusty loaf or a French loaf into small rounds or squares. Heat olive oil in a skillet and fry the slices until golden brown and crisp. Drain on paper towels.

SEAFOOD SALAD

Fresh seafood is plentiful in Italy and varieties of seafood salads are found all over the regions. Each has its own specialty, depending on availability and what appears in each day's catch.

STEP 1

SERVES 4

6 oz squid rings, defrosted if frozen
2½ cups water
⅔ cup dry white wine
⅓ cup hake or monkfish, cut into cubes
16-20 fresh mussels, scrubbed and beards
  removed
20 clams in shells, scrubbed, if available
  (otherwise use extra mussels)
⅓-1 cup peeled shrimp
3-4 scallions trimmed and sliced (optional)
radicchio and curly endive leaves, to serve
lemon wedges, to garnish

DRESSING
6 tbsp olive oil
1 tbsp wine vinegar
2 tbsp freshly chopped parsley
1-2 garlic cloves, crushed
salt and pepper

GARLIC MAYONNAISE
5 tbsp thick mayonnaise
2-3 tbsp fromage frais or plain yogurt
2 garlic cloves, crushed
1 tbsp capers
2 tbsp freshly chopped parsley or mixed
  herbs

1 Poach the squid in the water and wine for 20 minutes or until nearly tender. Add the fish cubes and continue to cook gently for 7-8 minutes or until tender. Strain, reserving the fish, and place the stock in a clean saucepan.

2 Bring the fish stock to the boil and add the mussels and clams. Cover the pot and simmer gently for about 5 minutes or until the shells open. Discard any that stay closed.

3 Drain the shellfish and remove from their shells. Put into a bowl with the cooked fish and add the shrimp and scallions, if using.

4 For the dressing, whisk together the oil, vinegar, parsley, garlic, salt and plenty of black pepper. Pour over the fish, mix well, cover, and chill for several hours.

5 Arrange small leaves of radicchio and curly endive on 4 plates and spoon the fish salad into the center. Garnish each plate with lemon wedges. Combine all the ingredients for the garlic mayonnaise and serve with the salad.

STEP 2

STEP 3

STEP 4

CHAPTER TWO

Pasta & Pizza

❧

It is well known that Italians are prolific eaters of pasta, but it may not be realized just how many varieties of pasta there are; in fact, it runs to many hundreds, and it would be almost impossible to list them all. Home-made pasta only takes a few minutes to cook while the dried variety takes longer, and it is best to follow the cooking directions on the package. If you are going to make a lot of pasta, it is well worth investing in a pasta-making machine, which will enable you to produce quantities with the minimum of effort.

Pasta is of Genoese origin but nowadays is even more popular in Naples and the southern regions of Italy; while in the north of the country a fair amount of rice is consumed. Milanese and other risottos are made with short-grain Italian rice, the best of which is Arborio, a type of rice that should never be rinsed before cooking. An Italian risotto is quite moist rice dish, but it should not be soggy or sticky.

Gnocchi are made from cornmeal, potato flour or semolina, often combined with spinach and some sort of cheese. They resemble dumplings, and are either poached or baked, and served with a cheese sauce. Polenta is made with either cornmeal or polenta flour and can be served either as a soft porridge or hard cake, which is then fried. The traditional method of making polenta involved long slow cooking, but now there is an excellent polenta mix that cuts the time to 5 minutes!

Opposite: The market in the Piazza della Fratta, Padua, offers a wide selection of fruit and vegetables. Italians like to shop daily, to make sure their produce is absolutely fresh.

STEP 2

STEP 3a

STEP 3b

STEP 4

TORTELLINI

According to legend, the shape of the tortellini is said to resemble the tummy button of Venus, but suffice to say that when you make tortellini from this description you know exactly what they should look like!

SERVES 4

FILLING
4 oz boneless, skinned chicken breast
2 oz prosciutto
2 tbsp cooked spinach, well drained
1 tbsp finely chopped onion
2 tbsp grated Parmesan
good pinch of ground allspice
1 egg, beaten
salt and pepper
1 quantity Pasta Dough (see page 76)

SAUCE:
1¼ cups light cream
1-2 garlic cloves, crushed
2 cups button mushrooms, thinly sliced
4 tbsp grated Parmesan
1-2 tbsp freshly chopped parsley

1 Poach the chicken in well-seasoned water until tender, about 10 minutes; drain and chop roughly. When cool put into a food processor with the prosciutto, spinach and onion, and process until finely chopped, then add the Parmesan, allspice, seasonings and egg.

2 Roll out the pasta dough, half at a time, on a lightly floured surface until as thin as possible. Cut into 1½-2-in circles using a plain cutter.

3 Place ½ teaspoon of the filling in the center of each dough circle, fold the pieces in half to make a semicircle and press the edges firmly together. Wrap the dough semicircle around your index finger and cross over the two ends, pressing firmly together, curling the rest of the dough backwards to make a "tummy button" shape. Slip the tortellini off your finger and lay on a lightly floured tray. Repeat with the rest of the dough, re-rolling the trimmings.

4 Cook the tortellini in batches: heat a large saucepan of salted boiling water and add some tortellini. Bring back to the boil and once they rise to the surface cook for about 5 minutes, giving an occasional stir. Remove with a slotted spoon, drain on paper towels, and keep warm in a serving dish while cooking the remainder.

5 To make the sauce, heat the cream with the garlic in a saucepan and bring to the boil; simmer for a few minutes. Add the mushrooms, half the Parmesan and seasoning and simmer for 2-3 minutes. Stir in the parsley and pour over the warm tortellini. Sprinkle the tortellini with the remaining Parmesan and serve immediately.

SICILIAN SPAGHETTI

This delicious Sicilian dish originated as a handy way of using up leftover cooked pasta. Any variety of long pasta could be used.

STEP 1

SERVES 4
OVEN: 400°F

2 eggplant, about 1¼ lb
⅔ cup olive oil
¾ lb lean ground beef
1 onion, peeled and chopped
2 garlic cloves, crushed
2 tbsp tomato paste
1 x 15-oz can peeled tomatoes, chopped
1 tsp Worcestershire sauce
1 tsp freshly chopped oregano or marjoram
   or ½ tsp dried oregano or marjoram
¼ cup pitted black olives, sliced
1 green, red or yellow bell pepper, cored,
   seeded and chopped
6 oz spaghetti
1 cup grated Parmesan
salt and pepper
oregano or parsley, to garnish (optional)

1 Brush an 8-in spring-mold cake pan with olive oil, place a disk of parchment paper in the base and oil. Trim the eggplant and cut into slanting slices about ¼ in thick. Heat some of the oil in a skillet. Fry a few slices at a time in hot oil until lightly browned, turning once, and adding more oil as necessary. Drain on paper towels.

2 Put the beef, onion and garlic into a saucepan and cook, stirring frequently, until browned all over. Add the tomato paste, tomatoes, Worcestershire sauce, herbs, and seasoning and simmer for 10 minutes, stirring occasionally, then add the olives and bell pepper and continue for a further 10 minutes.

3 Heat a large saucepan of salted water and cook the spaghetti for 12-14 minutes until tender. Drain thoroughly. Turn the spaghetti into a bowl and mix in the meat mixture and Parmesan, combining thoroughly using two forks.

4 Lay overlapping slices of eggplant evenly over the base of the cake pan and up the sides. Add the meat mixture, pressing it down, and cover with the remaining slices of eggplant.

5 Stand in a baking pan and cook in a preheated oven for 40 minutes. Leave to stand for 5 minutes then loosen around the edges and invert onto a warmed serving dish, releasing the spring. Remove the paper. Sprinkle with herbs before serving, if liked. Extra Parmesan cheese may also be offered.

STEP 3

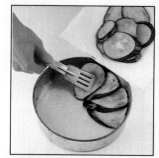

STEP 4a

STEP 4b

GNOCCHI ROMANA

This is a traditional recipe from Piedmont. For a less rich version, omit the eggs. It is often served as a first course before a light main course, but it makes an excellent main meal with a crisp salad.

STEP 1

SERVES 4
OVEN: 400°F

3 cups milk
¼ tsp grated nutmeg
6 tbsp butter, plus extra for greasing
1⅓ cups semolina
1 cup Parmesan, finely grated
2 eggs, beaten
½ cup Gruyère, grated
salt and pepper
basil sprigs, to garnish

1 Bring the milk to the boil, remove from the heat and stir in seasoning, nutmeg and 2 tablespoons butter. Gradually whisk in the semolina to prevent lumps forming and return to a low heat. Simmer gently for about 10 minutes, stirring constantly, until very thick.

2 Beat ½ cup of Parmesan into the semolina, followed by the eggs. Continue beating until it is quite smooth.

3 Spread out the semolina mixture in an even layer on a sheet of parchment paper or in a large oiled baking pan, smoothing the surface with a wet spatula – it should be about ½ in

STEP 2

thick. Leave until cold, then chill for about an hour until firm.

4 Cut the gnocchi into circles of about 1½ in, using a plain greased pastry cutter.

5 Thoroughly grease a shallow ovenproof dish, or 4 individual dishes. Lay the gnocchi trimmings in the base of the dish and cover with overlapping circles of gnocchi. Melt the remaining butter and drizzle all over the gnocchi, then sprinkle first with the remaining Parmesan and then with the grated Gruyère.

6 Cook in a preheated oven for 25-30 minutes until the top is crisp and golden brown.

STEP 3

NOTE

Tomato and Pepper Sauce (see page 17) may be served with this dish.

STEP 4

POLENTA

Polenta is prepared in a variety of ways and can be served hot or cold, sweet or savoury. This is the traditional way of making it in Lombardy, although there is now an instant polenta mix available.

STEP 1

SERVES 4

7 cups water
1¹/₂ tsp salt
2 cups polenta or cornmeal flour
2 beaten eggs (optional)
2 cups fresh fine white breadcrumbs
*   (optional)*
vegetable oil, for frying and oiling

MUSHROOM SAUCE
4 cups mushrooms, sliced
3 tbsp olive oil
2 garlic cloves, crushed
²/₃ cup dry white wine
4 tbsp heavy cream
2 tbsp freshly chopped mixed herbs
salt and pepper

1 Bring the water and salt to the boil in a large saucepan and gradually sprinkle in the polenta or cornmeal, stirring all the time to make sure the mixture is smooth and there are no lumps.

2 Simmer the mixture very gently, stirring frequently, until the polenta becomes very thick, about 30-35 minutes. It is likely to splatter, in which case partially cover the pot with a lid.

STEP 2

The mixture should become thick enough for a wooden spoon to almost stand upright in it on its own.

3 Thoroughly oil a shallow pan, about 11 x 7 in, and spoon in the polenta. Spread out evenly, using a wet spatula if necessary. Leave until cold, then leave for a few hours at room temperature, if possible.

4 Cut the polenta into 30-36 squares. Heat the oil in a skillet and fry the pieces until golden brown all over, turning several times – about 5 minutes. Alternatively, dip each piece of polenta in beaten egg and coat in breadcrumbs before frying in the hot oil.

5 To make the mushroom sauce: heat the oil in a saucepan and fry the mushrooms with the crushed garlic for 3-4 minutes. Add the wine, season well and simmer for 5 minutes. Add the cream and chopped herbs and simmer for another minute or so.

6 Serve the polenta with the mushroom sauce. It could also be served with a tomato sauce, if preferred.

STEP 3

STEP 4

TAGLIATELLE WITH PUMPKIN

This unusual pasta dish comes from Emilia Romagna.

STEP 1

STEP 2

STEP 3a

STEP 3b

SERVES 4

1 lb pumpkin or butternut squash
2 tbsp olive oil
1 onion, peeled and finely chopped
2 garlic cloves, crushed
4-6 tbsp freshly chopped parsley
good pinch of ground or grated nutmeg
about 1 cup chicken or vegetable stock
4 oz prosciutto, cut into narrow strips
9 oz tagliatelle, green or white (fresh or
    dried)
²/₃ cup heavy cream
salt and pepper
freshly grated Parmesan, to serve

1 Peel the pumpkin or butternut squash, removing the hard layer directly under the skin and scoop out the seeds and membrane around them. Cut the flesh into ½-in dice.

2 Heat the oil in a saucepan and fry the onion and garlic gently until soft. Add half the parsley and continue for a minute or so longer.

3 Add the pumpkin or squash and continue to cook for 2-3 minutes,

then season well with salt, pepper, and nutmeg and add half the stock. Bring to the boil, cover, and simmer for about 10 minutes or until the pumpkin is tender, adding more stock as necessary. Add the prosciutto and continue to cook for a further 2 minutes, stirring frequently.

4 Meanwhile, cook the tagliatelle in a large saucepan of boiling salted water, allowing 3-4 minutes for fresh pasta or about 12 minutes for dried (or follow the directions on the package). When *al dente*, drain thoroughly and turn into a warmed dish.

5 Add the cream to the ham mixture and heat gently until really hot. Adjust the seasoning and spoon over the pasta. Sprinkle with the remaining parsley and pass around the grated Parmesan cheese separately.

FRESH PASTA

If you want to make your own pasta, use the recipe for pasta dough (see page 76), roll it out as thinly as possible and cut into narrow strips. Allow to dry on a cloth over a rack before cooking.

STEP 1

STEP 2

STEP 4

STEP 5

MILANESE RISOTTO

Italian rice is a round, short-grained variety with a nutty flavor, which is essential for a good risotto. Arborio is the very best kind to use.

SERVES 4-5

2 good pinches of saffron threads
1 large onion, finely chopped
1-2 garlic cloves, crushed
6 tbsp butter
1²/₃ cups Arborio or other short-grain
    Italian rice
²/₃ cup dry white wine
5 cups boiling stock (chicken, beef or
    vegetable)
³/₄ cup grated Parmesan
salt and pepper

1 Put the saffron in a small bowl, cover with 3-4 tablespoons boiling water, and leave to soak while cooking the risotto.

2 Fry the onion and garlic in 4 tablespoons of the butter until soft but not colored, then add the rice and continue to cook for a few minutes until all the grains are coated in oil and beginning to color lightly.

3 Add the wine to the rice and simmer gently, stirring from time to time until it is all absorbed.

4 Add the boiling stock a little at a time, about ⅔ cup, cooking until

the liquid is fully absorbed before adding more, and stirring frequently.

5 When all the stock is absorbed the rice should be tender but not soft or soggy. Add the saffron liquid, Parmesan, remaining butter, and plenty of seasoning and simmer for a minute or so until piping hot and thoroughly mixed.

6 Cover the saucepan tightly and leave to stand for 5 minutes off the heat. Give a good stir and serve at once.

COOKING RISOTTO

The finished dish should have moist but separate grains. This is achieved by adding the hot stock a little at a time, only adding more when the last addition is fully absorbed. Don't leave the risotto to cook by itself: it needs constant watching to see when more liquid is required.

STEP 1

STEP 2

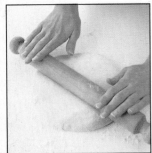

STEP 3a

STEP 3b

CALABRIAN PIZZA

Traditionally, a Calabrian pizza has a double layer of dough to make it robust and filling. It can be made as a single pizza (as shown here). Use the second piece of dough for another base and double the filling.

SERVES 4-6
OVEN: 350°F

3½ cups all-purpose flour
½ tsp salt
1 package acive dry yeast
2 tbsp olive oil
about 1 cup warm water

FILLING:
2 tbsp olive oil
2 garlic cloves, crushed
1 red bell pepper, cored, seeded and sliced
1 yellow bell pepper, cored, seeded and sliced
½ cup ricotta
¾ cup sun-dried tomatoes, drained
3 hard-boiled eggs, thinly sliced
1 tbsp freshly chopped mixed herbs
4 oz salami, cut into strips
5-6 oz mozzarella, grated
a little milk, to glaze
salt and pepper

1 Sift the flour and salt into a bowl and mix in the yeast, then add the olive oil and enough warm water to mix to a smooth pliable dough. Knead for 10-15 minutes by hand, or process for 5 minutes in a mixer fitted with a dough hook.

2 Shape the dough into a ball, place in a lightly oiled plastic bag, and put in a warm place for 1-1½ hours or until doubled in size.

3 For the filling: heat the oil in a skillet and fry the garlic and bell peppers slowly in the oil until soft. Punch down the dough and roll out half to fit the base of a 12 x 10 in oiled roasting pan. Season the dough and spread with the ricotta, then cover with sun-dried tomatoes, hard-boiled eggs, herbs and the pepper mixture. Arrange the salami strips on top and sprinkle with the grated cheese.

4 Roll out the remaining dough and place over the filling, pressing the edges well together, or use to make a second pizza. Put to rise for about an hour in a warm place until well puffed up. An uncovered pizza will only take about 30-40 minutes to rise.

5 Prick the double pizza with a fork about 20 times, brush the top with milk and cook in a preheated oven for about 50 minutes or until lightly browned and firm to the touch. The uncovered pizza will take only 35-40 minutes. Serve hot.

CHAPTER THREE

Fish & Shellfish

❦

Italians eat everything that comes out of the sea, from the smallest whitebait to the massive tuna fish, not forgetting the wide variety of shellfish. Fish markets in Italy are fascinating, with a huge variety of fish on display, but as most of their fish comes from the Mediterranean it is not always easy to find an equivalent elsewhere. However, imported frozen fish of all kinds is now appearing in supermarkets. After pasta, fish is probably the most important source of food in Italy, and in many recipes fish or shellfish is combined with some type of pasta. The inland regions of Italy, such as Lombardy and Umbria have lakes with plentiful supplies of fish while Apulia has abundant supples caught by offshore trawlers. The South has splendid fish, with tuna and swordfish taking pride of place, although red mullet and sea bass are plentiful and popular too. Venice and surrounding areas have a wealth of fish and shellfish recipes, often combined with pasta, while the Ligurian coast is popular for fish soups and stews. The islands of Sicily and Sardinia abound with fish, which feature widely in their cuisine, from the large tuna to the sardines that give Sardinia its name.

Opposite: The fishing fleet prepares to set off in the early morning light. Later in the day the catch – anything from John Dory, bass, mullet, snapper and squid to lobsters and crabs – will be proudly displayed on the quayside, ready for the market.

STEP 2a

STEP 2b

STEP 4a

STEP 4b

BAKED SEA BASS

*Sea bass is a delicious white-fleshed fish with a wonderful fresh flavor.
If cooking 2 small fish, they can be broiled; if cooking
one large fish, bake it in the oven.*

SERVES 4
OVEN: 375°F

3 lb fresh sea bass or 2 x 1½-lb sea bass,
   gutted
2-4 sprigs fresh rosemary
½ lemon, thinly sliced
2 tbsp olive oil

GARLIC SAUCE:
2 tsp coarse sea salt
2 tsp capers
2 garlic cloves, crushed
4 tbsp water
2 fresh bay leaves
1 tsp lemon juice or wine vinegar
2 tbsp olive oil
black pepper
bay leaves and lemon wedges, to garnish

1 Scrape off the scales from the fish
and cut off the sharp fins. Make
diagonal cuts along both sides. Wash
and dry thoroughly.

2 Place a sprig of rosemary in the
cavity of each of the smaller fish
with half the lemon slices; or 2 sprigs
and all the lemon in the large fish. To
broil, place in a foil-lined pan, brush
lightly with 1-2 tablespoons oil and broil

under a moderate heat for about 5
minutes each side or until cooked
through, turning carefully.

3 To bake: place the fish in a foil-lined
dish or roasting pan brushed with
oil, and brush the fish with the rest of the
oil. Cook in a preheated oven for about
30 minutes for the small fish or 45-50
minutes for the large fish, until tender
when tested with a skewer.

4 For the sauce: crush the salt and
capers with the garlic in a pestle
and mortar if available and then
gradually work in the water.
Alternatively, put it all into a food
processor or blender and switch on until
smooth. Bruise the bay leaves and
remaining sprigs of rosemary and put in
a bowl. Add the garlic mixture, lemon
juice or vinegar and oil and pound
together until the flavors are released.
Season with black pepper.

5 Place the fish on a serving dish and,
if liked, carefully remove the skin.
Spoon some of the sauce over the fish and
serve the rest separately. Garnish with
fresh bay leaves and lemon wedges.

STEP 2

STEP 4

STEP 5a

STEP 5b

SARDINE & POTATO BAKE

Fresh sardines bear very little resemblance to the canned varieties. They are now available frozen, and sometimes fresh, so this traditional dish from Liguria can now be enjoyed by all.

SERVES 4
OVEN: 375°F

2 lb potatoes, peeled
2 lb sardines, defrosted if frozen
1 tbsp olive oil, plus extra for oiling
1 onion, peeled and chopped
2-3 garlic cloves, crushed
2 tbsp freshly chopped parsley
12 oz ripe tomatoes, peeled and sliced or
 1 x 15-oz can peeled tomatoes, partly
 drained and chopped
1-2 tbsp freshly chopped Italian herbs (e.g.
 oregano, thyme, rosemary, marjoram)
²/₃ cup dry white wine
salt and pepper

1 Put the potatoes in a saucepan of salted water, bring to the boil, cover and simmer for 10 minutes, then drain. When cool enough to handle, cut into slices about ¼ in thick.

2 Gut and clean the sardines: cut off their heads and tails and then slit open the length of the belly. Turn the fish over so the skin is upwards and press firmly along the backbone to loosen the bones. Turn over again and carefully remove the backbone. Wash the fish in cold water, drain well and dry them on paper towels.

3 Heat the oil in a skillet and fry the onion and garlic until soft, but not colored.

4 Arrange the potatoes in a well-oiled ovenproof dish and sprinkle with the onions and then the parsley and plenty of seasoning.

5 Lay the open sardines over the potatoes, skin-side down, then cover with the tomatoes and the rest of the herbs. Pour on the wine and season again.

6 Cook uncovered in a preheated oven for about 40 minutes until the fish is tender. If the casserole seems to be drying out, add another couple of tablespoons of wine.

V A R I A T I O N

Fresh anchovies may be used in this recipe in place of sardines. Prepare in the same way.

TROUT IN RED WINE

This recipe from Trentino is best when the fish are freshly caught, but it is a good way to cook any trout, giving it an interesting flavor and succulent flesh.

STEP 1

STEP 3

STEP 4

STEP 5

SERVES 4

4 fresh trout, about 10 oz each
1 cup red or white wine vinegar
1¼ cups red or dry white wine
⅔ cup water
1 carrot, peeled and sliced
2-4 bay leaves
thinly pared rind of 1 lemon
1 small onion, peeled and very thinly sliced
4 sprigs fresh parsley
4 sprigs fresh thyme
1 tsp black peppercorns
6-8 whole cloves
6 tbsp butter
1 tbsp freshly chopped mixed herbs or
   parsley
salt and pepper
herbs and lemon slices, to garnish

1 Gut the trout but leave their heads on. Dry on paper towels and lay the fish head to tail in a shallow container just large enough to hold them.

2 Bring the wine vinegar to the boil and pour slowly all over the fish. Leave the fish to marinate for about 20 minutes.

3 Put the wine, water, carrot, bay leaves, lemon rind, onion, herbs, peppercorns, and cloves into a saucepan with a good pinch of sea salt and heat gently.

4 Drain the fish thoroughly, discarding the vinegar. Place the fish in a fish kettle or large skillet so they touch. When the wine mixture boils, strain gently over the fish so they are about half covered. Cover, and simmer very gently for 15 minutes.

5 Carefully remove the fish from the liquid, draining off as much as possible, and arrange on a serving dish.

6 Boil the cooking liquid hard until reduced to about 4-6 tablespoons. Melt the butter in a small saucepan and strain in the cooking liquor. Adjust the seasoning and spoon over the fish. Sprinkle with chopped mixed herbs and garnish with lemon and sprigs of herbs.

STEP 1a

STEP 1b

STEP 2

STEP 3

SQUID CASSEROLE

Squid and octopus are great favorites in Italy and around the Mediterranean resorts. Squid is often served fried, but here it is casseroled with tomatoes and bell peppers to give a rich sauce.

SERVES 4
OVEN: 350°F

2 lb whole squid or 1½ lb squid rings,
 defrosted if frozen
3 tbsp olive oil
1 large onion, thinly sliced
2 garlic cloves, crushed
1 red bell pepper, cored, seeded and sliced
1-2 sprigs fresh rosemary
²⁄₃ cup dry white wine and 1 cup water, or
 1½ cups water or fish stock
1 x 15-oz can peeled tomatoes, chopped
2 tbsp tomato paste
1 tsp paprika
salt and pepper
fresh sprigs of rosemary or parsley, to
 garnish

1 Prepare the squid (see right) and cut into ½-in slices; cut the tentacles into lengths of about 2 in. If using frozen squid rings, make sure they are fully defrosted and well drained.

2 Heat the oil in a flameproof casserole and fry the onion and garlic gently until soft. Add the squid rings, increase the heat and continue to cook for about 10 minutes until sealed

and beginning to color lightly. Add the red bell pepper, rosemary and wine (if using), and water or stock and bring up to the boil. Cover and simmer gently for 45 minutes.

3 Discard the sprigs of rosemary (but don't take out any leaves that have come off). Add the tomatoes, tomato paste, seasonings, and paprika. Continue to simmer gently for 45-60 minutes, or cover the casserole tightly and cook in a moderate oven for 45-60 minutes until tender.

4 Give the sauce a good stir, adjust the seasoning and serve with crusty bread.

TO PREPARE SQUID

Peel off as much as possible of the fine outer skin, using your fingers, then cut off the head and tentacles. Extract the transparent flat oval bone from the body and discard. Carefully remove the sac of black ink, then turn the body sac inside out. Wash thoroughly in cold water. Cut off the tentacles from the head and discard the rest; wash thoroughly.

CHAPTER FOUR

Meat & Poultry

❦

Italians tend to have their own special way of butchering meat, producing very different cuts. Most of their meat is sold ready boned and often cut straight across the grain. They tend to serve prime cuts and steaks very rare, so great care needs to be taken when ordering in a restaurant. Veal is a great favorite in Italy and widely available, with the popular cuts for scallops always made straight across the grain of the meat. It is then beaten out thinly, using a meat mallet. Pork is also popular, with roast pig the traditional dish of Umbria. Suckling pig is roasted with lots of fresh herbs, especially rosemary, until the skin is crisp and brown. Lamb is often served for special occasions, cooked on a spit or roasted in the oven with wine, garlic and herbs; and the very small cutlets from young lambs feature widely, especially in Rome. Variety meats play an important role in Italian cooking, with liver, brains, sweetbreads, tongue, heart, tripe and kidneys, from both veal and lamb, always available. Poultry dishes provide some of Italy's finest food. Every part of the chicken is used, including the feet and innards for making soup. Spit-roasted chicken, flavored strongly with rosemary, has become almost a national Italian dish. Turkey, capon, duck, goose and guinea fowl are also popular, as is game. Wild rabbit and hare, wild boar, and deer are also available, especially in Sardinia.

Opposite: *Italians take their food very seriously, so eating out is a very popular activity. Blessed with a wonderful climate, they can often eat outdoors, as in this Venetian restaurant.*

PIZZAIOLA STEAK

This has a Neapolitan sauce, using the delicious red tomatoes so abundant in that area, but canned ones make an excellent alternative.

STEP 3

SERVES 4

2 x 15-oz cans peeled tomatoes or 1½ lb
  fresh tomatoes
4 tbsp olive oil
2-3 garlic cloves, crushed
1 onion, finely chopped
1 tbsp tomato paste
1½ tsp freshly chopped marjoram or
  oregano or ¾ tsp dried marjoram or
  oregano
4 thin sirloin or rump steaks
2 tbsp freshly chopped parsley
1 tsp sugar
salt and pepper
fresh herbs, to garnish (optional)
sauté potatoes, to serve

1 If using canned tomatoes, purée them in a food processor, then sieve to remove the seeds. If using fresh tomatoes, peel, remove the seeds, and chop finely.

2 Heat half the oil in a saucepan and fry the garlic and onions very gently until soft – about 5 minutes.

3 Add the tomatoes, seasoning, tomato paste and chopped herbs. If using fresh tomatoes, add 4 tablespoons water too, and then simmer very gently

STEP 4

for 8-10 minutes, giving an occasional stir.

4 Meanwhile, trim the steaks if necessary and season with salt and pepper. Heat the remaining oil in a skillet and fry the steaks quickly on both sides to seal, then continue until cooked to your liking – 2 minutes for rare, 3-4 minutes for medium, or 5 minutes for well done. Alternatively, cook the steaks under a hot broiler after brushing lightly with oil.

5 When the sauce has thickened a little, adjust the seasoning and stir in the chopped parsley and sugar to taste.

STEP 5

6 Pour off the excess fat from the pan with the steaks and add the tomato sauce. Reheat gently and serve at once, with the sauce spooned over and around the steaks. Garnish with fresh herbs, if liked. Sauté potatoes make a good accompaniment with a green vegetable.

ALTERNATIVE

This sauce can be served with veal and chicken. It can also be served with broiled or baked white fish.

STEP 6

STEP 1

STEP 2

STEP 3

STEP 4

VITELLO TONNATO

Veal dishes are the specialty of Lombardy, with this dish being one of the more sophisticated. Serve cold, either as part of an antipasta or as a main course. It is best served with seasonal salads.

SERVES 4

1¹/₂ lb boned leg of veal, rolled
2 bay leaves
10 black peppercorns
2-3 whole cloves
¹/₂ tsp salt
2 carrots, sliced
1 onion, sliced
2 celery sticks, sliced
about 3 cups stock or water
²/₃ cup dry white wine (optional)
3 oz canned tuna fish, well drained
1 x 1¹/₂ oz can anchovy fillets, drained
²/₃ cup olive oil
2 tsp bottled capers, drained
2 egg yolks
1 tbsp lemon juice
salt and pepper

TO GARNISH:
capers
lemon wedges
fresh herbs

1 Put the veal in a saucepan with the bay leaves, peppercorns, cloves, salt, and vegetables. Add sufficient stock or water and the wine (if using) to barely cover the veal. Bring to the boil, remove any scum from the surface, then cover the pot and simmer gently for an hour or so until tender. Leave in the water until cold, then drain thoroughly. If time allows, chill the veal to make it easier to carve.

2 For the tuna sauce: thoroughly mash the tuna fish with 4 anchovy fillets and 1 tablespoon oil and the capers, then add the egg yolks and press through a sieve or purée in a food processor or liquidizer until smooth.

3 Stir in the lemon juice, then gradually whisk in the rest of the oil a few drops at a time until the sauce is smooth and has the consistency of thick cream. Season to taste.

4 Slice the veal thinly and arrange on a flat platter in overlapping slices. Spoon the tunafish sauce over the veal to cover. Then cover the dish and chill overnight.

5 Before serving, uncover the veal carefully. Arrange the remaining anchovy fillets and the capers in a decorative pattern on top, and garnish with lemon wedges and herbs.

STEP 1

STEP 3

STEP 4

STEP 6

POT ROAST LEG OF LAMB

This dish from the Abruzzi is even better if you use a leg of mutton in place of lamb: the meat absorbs the flavors even better and becomes very tender, giving a truly memorable dish.

SERVES 4
OVEN: 350°F

3½-lb leg of lamb
3-4 sprigs fresh rosemary
4 slices bacon
4 tbsp olive oil
2-3 garlic cloves, crushed
2 onions, sliced
2 carrots, sliced
2 celery sticks, sliced
1¼ cups dry white wine
1 tbsp tomato paste
1¼ cups stock
12 oz tomatoes, peeled, quartered and seeded
1 tbsp freshly chopped parsley
1 tbsp freshly chopped oregano or marjoram
salt and pepper
fresh rosemary sprigs, to garnish

1 Wipe the lamb all over, trimming off any excess fat, then season well with salt and pepper, rubbing well in. Lay the sprigs of rosemary over the lamb, cover evenly with the bacon and tie in place with fine string.

2 Heat the oil in a skillet and fry the lamb until browned all over, turning several times – about 10 minutes. Remove from the pan.

3 Transfer the oil from the skillet to a large fireproof casserole and fry the garlic and onion together for 3-4 minutes until beginning to soften, then add the carrots and celery and continue to cook for a few minutes longer.

4 Lay the lamb on top of the vegetables and press well to partly bury. Pour the wine over the lamb, add the tomato paste and simmer for 3-4 minutes. Add the stock, tomatoes, and herbs and plenty of seasoning and bring back to the boil for a further 3-4 minutes.

5 Cover the casserole tightly and cook in a moderate oven for 2-2½ hours until very tender.

6 Remove the lamb from the casserole and, if liked, take off the bacon and herbs along with the string. Keep warm. Strain the juices, skimming off any excess fat, and serve separately. The vegetables may be put around the meat or in a serving dish. Garnish with fresh sprigs of rosemary.

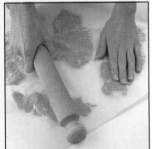

STEP 2

STEP 3

STEP 4

STEP 5

SALTIMBOCCA

*Literally translated saltimbocca means "jump in the mouth",
and this quick, tasty veal dish almost does that.*

SERVES 4

4 thin veal scallops
8 fresh sage leaves
4 thin slices prosciutto (same size as
   the veal)
flour, for dredging
2 tbsp olive oil
2 tbsp butter
4 tbsp white wine
4 tbsp chicken stock
4 tbsp marsala
salt and pepper
fresh sage leaves, to garnish

1 Either leave the scallops as they are or cut in half. Place the pieces of veal on a sheet of plastic wrap or parchment paper, keeping well apart, and cover with another piece.

2 Using a meat mallet or rolling pin, beat the veal gently until at least twice the size and very thin.

3 Lightly season the veal with salt and pepper and lay 2 fresh sage leaves on the large slices, or 1 on each of the smaller slices. Then lay the prosciutto slices evenly over the meat to cover the sage and fit the size of the veal almost exactly.

4 Secure the prosciutto to the veal with wooden toothpicks. If preferred, the large slices can be folded in half first. Dredge lightly with a little flour.

5 Heat the olive oil and butter in a large skillet and fry the meat until golden brown each side and just cooked through – about 4 minutes for single slices or 5-6 minutes for double ones. Take care not to overcook. Remove to a serving dish and keep warm.

6 Add the wine, stock, and marsala to the skillet and bring to the boil, stirring well to loosen all the sediment. Boil until reduced by almost half. Adjust the seasoning and quickly pour over the saltimbocca. Serve at once, garnished with fresh sage leaves.

ALTERNATIVE

This dish can also be made using boneless chicken breasts. Slit the breasts almost in half, open out and beat as thinly as possible, as for the veal.

CHICKEN WITH GREEN OLIVES

Olives are a popular flavoring for poultry and game in Apulia, where this recipe originates. In Italy every morsel of the bird is used in some way, most often for soups and stock.

STEP 1

SERVES 4
OVEN: 350°F

4 chicken breasts, part boned
2 tbsp butter
2 tbsp olive oil
1 large onion, finely chopped
2 garlic cloves, crushed
2 bell peppers, red, yellow or green, cored, seeded and cut into large pieces
4 cups large closed cup mushrooms, sliced or quartered
6 oz tomatoes, peeled and halved
²/₃ cup dry white wine
²/₃-1 cup cup green olives, pitted
4-6 tbsp heavy cream
salt and pepper
flat-leaf parsley, chopped, to garnish

1 Season the chicken with salt and pepper. Heat the oil and butter in a skillet, add the chicken and fry until browned all over. Remove from the pan.

2 Add the onion and garlic to the skillet and fry gently until beginning to soften. Add the bell peppers with the mushrooms and continue to cook for a few minutes longer.

3 Add the tomatoes and plenty of seasoning and then transfer the vegetable mixture to an ovenproof casserole. Place the chicken on the bed of vegetables.

4 Add the wine to the skillet and bring to the boil. Pour the wine over the chicken and cover the casserole tightly. Cook in a preheated oven for 50 minutes.

5 Add the olives to the chicken, mix lightly, then pour on the cream. Re-cover the casserole and return to the oven for 10-20 minutes or until the chicken is very tender.

6 Adjust the seasoning and serve the pieces of chicken, surrounded by the vegetables and sauce, with pasta or tiny new potatoes. Sprinkle with parsley to garnish.

STEP 2

STEP 3

NOODLES

Serve this dish with freshly made ribbon noodles for a really attractive presentation. Fresh pasta takes only 2-3 minutes to cook.

STEP 5

LIVER WITH WINE SAUCE

Liver is popular in Italy and is served in many ways. The ideal is calf's liver, but lamb's liver is a delicious and common alternative.

STEP 1

STEP 2

STEP 3

SERVES 4

4 slices calf's liver or 8 slices lamb's liver, about 1 lb
flour, for coating
1 tbsp olive oil
2 tbsp butter
1 garlic clove, crushed
4 lean bacon slices
1 onion, chopped
1 celery stick, thinly sliced
²/₃ cup red wine
²/₃ cup beef stock
good pinch of ground allspice
1 tsp Worcestershire sauce
1 tsp freshly chopped sage or ¹/₂ tsp dried sage
3-4 tomatoes, peeled
salt and pepper
fresh sage leaves, to garnish
sauté potatoes, to serve

1 Wipe the liver, season with salt and pepper and coat lightly in flour, shaking off the surplus.

2 Heat the oil and butter in a skillet and fry the liver until well sealed on both sides and just cooked through – take care not to overcook. Remove the liver from the skillet, cover and keep warm, but do not allow to dry out.

3 Cut the bacon into narrow strips and add to the fat left in the skillet with the onion and celery. Fry gently until soft.

4 Add the wine and stock, allspice, Worcestershire sauce and seasonings, bring to the boil and simmer for 3-4 minutes.

5 Quarter the tomatoes, discard the seeds and cut each piece in half. Add to the sauce and continue to cook for a couple of minutes.

6 Serve the liver on a little of the sauce, with the remainder spooned over. Garnish with fresh sage leaves and serve with tiny new potatoes or sauté potatoes.

COOKING LIVER

Overcooked liver is dry and tasteless, especially when it is coated in flour. Cook the slices for only 2-3 minutes on each side – they should be soft and tender, and still a little pink in the center.

STEP 4

CHAPTER FIVE

Desserts

❦

Many Italians prefer to finish their meal with a bowl of mixed fruits or fruits with cheese, but they do like their desserts too. When there is a family gathering or a celebration, then a special effort is made and the delicacies appear. The Sicilians are said to have the sweetest tooth of all, and many Italian desserts are thought to have originated there. Ice cream (*gelato*), sorbet and water ice (*granita*) are said to be borrowed from the Arabs, who occupied Sicily centuries ago, and you have to go a very long way to beat a Sicilian ice cream, especially the famous cassata and ricotta ice creams. Fruits feature in desserts too. The famous pear tarts of the north are mouthwatering, using the very best fruit blended with apricot jam, raisins and almonds, while oranges appear marinated in syrup and liqueur. Cookies with almond flavoring are often served as an accompaniment, and the famous florentines – cookies full of glacé fruit and covered with chocolate – are favorites too. Cakes are popular, often incorporating ricotta cheese along with citrus fruits and honey. Tiramisu is a favorite with all, and for Christmas and special occasions try the honey cake from Siena called Panforte – so very rich that even a tiny piece will leave you with delicious memories for a very long time.

Opposite: The fertile plains of Tuscany grow an enormous variety of fruit and vegetables. Many famous desserts originate here, including the luscious Panforte di Siena.

STEP 1a

STEP 1b

STEP 2

STEP 5

TIRAMISU

A favorite Italian dessert which is found in many regions. Here it is flavored with coffee and Amaretto, but you could also use marsala and maraschino.

SERVES 4-6

20-24 ladyfingers
2 tbsp cold black coffee
2 tbsp coffee essence
2 tbsp Amaretto or brandy
4 egg yolks
6 tbsp superfine sugar
few drops of vanilla essence
grated rind of ¹/₂ lemon
1¹/₂ cups mascarpone cheese or ³/₄ cup heavy
*   cream and ³/₄ cup cream cheese, beaten*
*   together*
2 tsp lemon juice
1 cup heavy cream
1 tbsp milk
¹/₄ cup flaked almonds, lightly toasted
2 tbsp cocoa powder
1 tbsp confectioners' sugar

1 Arrange almost half the ladyfingers in the base of a glass bowl or serving dish. Combine the black coffee, coffee essence and Amaretto or brandy and sprinkle just over half the mixture on top.

2 Put the egg yolks into a heatproof bowl with the sugar, vanilla essence, and lemon rind. Place the bowl over a saucepan of gently simmering water and whisk until very thick and creamy and the whisk leaves a very heavy trail when lifted from the bowl.

3 Put the mascarpone cheese into a bowl, add the lemon juice and beat until smooth.

4 Combine the egg mixture and mascarpone cheese. When evenly blended pour half over the ladyfingers and spread out evenly.

5 Add another layer of ladyfingers, sprinkle with the remaining coffee, and then cover with the rest of the cheese mixture. Chill for at least 2 hours and preferably longer, or overnight.

6 To serve, whip the cream and milk together until fairly stiff and spread or pipe over the dessert. Sprinkle with the flaked almonds and then sift an even layer of cocoa powder so the top is completely covered. Finally sift a very light layer of confectioners' sugar over the cocoa.

ZABAGLIONE

This light, sweet dessert is reminiscent of a whisked egg custard. Serve warm or chilled, accompanied by ladyfingers or amaretti cookies, and soft fruits such as strawberries or raspberries.

STEP 1

SERVES 4

6 egg yolks
6 tbsp superfine sugar
6 tbsp marsala
ladyfingers or amaretti cookies, to serve
strawberries or raspberries, to decorate
    (optional)

1 Put the egg yolks into a heatproof bowl and whisk until a pale yellow color, using a rotary, balloon or electric whisk.

2 Whisk in the sugar, followed by the marsala, continuing to whisk all the time.

3 Stand the bowl over a saucepan of very gently simmering water, or transfer to the top of a double boiler, and continue to whisk continuously. Whisk until the mixture thickens sufficiently to stand in soft peaks. On no account allow the water to boil or the zabaglione will overcook and turn into scrambled eggs.

4 Scrape around the sides of the bowl from time to time while whisking. As soon as the mixture is really thick and foamy, take from the heat and continue to whisk for a couple of minutes longer.

5 Pour immediately into stemmed glasses and serve warm; or leave until cold and serve chilled.

6 Fruits such as strawberries or raspberries, or crumbled ladyfingers or amaretti cookies may be placed in the base of the glasses before adding the zabaglione.

STEP 2

STEP 3

STEP 4

ALTERNATIVE

Any other type of liqueur may be used in place of marsala.

67

PANFORTE DI SIENA

This famous Tuscan honey and nut cake is a Christmas specialty. In Italy it is sold in pretty boxes, which seems to make it taste even better. Panforte is very rich and sticky and should be served in very thin slices.

STEP 1

STEP 2

STEP 3

STEP 5

SERVES 12
OVEN: 300°F

1 cup split whole almonds
¾ cup hazelnuts
½ cup cut mixed peel
⅓ cup no-need-to-soak dried apricots
⅓ cup glacé or crystallized pineapple
grated rind of 1 large orange
½ cup all-purpose flour
2 tbsp cocoa powder
2 tsp ground cinnamon
½ cup superfine sugar
½ cup honey
confectioners' sugar

1 Toast the almonds until lightly browned and place in a bowl. Toast the hazelnuts under the broiler until the skins split. Place the hazelnuts on a dish towel and rub off the skins with the towel. Roughly chop the hazelnuts and add to the almonds with the mixed peel.

2 Chop the apricots and pineapple fairly finely, add to the nuts with the orange rind and mix well.

3 Sift the flour with the cocoa and cinnamon, add to the nut mixture and mix evenly.

4 Line a round 8-in cake pan with parchment paper.

5 Put the sugar and honey into a saucepan and heat until the sugar dissolves, then boil gently for about 5 minutes or until the mixture thickens and begins to turn a deeper shade of brown. Quickly add to the nut mixture and stir through it evenly. Turn into the prepared pan and level the top with the help of a damp spoon.

6 Cook in a cool oven for an hour. Remove from the oven and leave in the pan until cold. Take out of the pan and carefully peel off the paper. Before serving, cover the cake heavily with sifted confectioners' sugar. Serve cut into very thin slices.

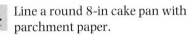

STORAGE

Panforte will keep for several weeks stored in an airtight container or securely wrapped in foil.

PEAR TART

Pears are a very popular fruit in Italy. In this recipe from Trentino they are flavored with almonds, cinnamon, raisins and apricot jam, then baked in an open tart with a soft-textured sweet pastry.

STEP 1

SERVES 4-6
OVEN: 400°F

2¼ cups all-purpose flour
pinch of salt
½ cup superfine sugar
½ cup butter, diced
1 egg
1 egg yolk
few drops of vanilla essence
2-3 tsp water

FILLING:
4 tbsp apricot jam
½ cup amaretti or ratafia cookies, crumbled
1¾-2 lb pears, peeled and cored
1 tsp ground cinnamon
½ cup raisins
⅓ cup soft brown sugar
sifted confectioners' sugar, for sprinkling

1 Sift the flour and salt onto a flat surface, make a well in the center and add the sugar, butter, egg, egg yolk, vanilla essence, and most of the water.

2 Using your fingers, gradually work the flour into the other ingredients to give a smooth, pliable dough, adding a little more water, if necessary. Wrap in plastic wrap and chill for an hour or until firm. Alternatively, put all the ingredients into a food processor and process until evenly blended and smooth.

3 Using almost ¾ of the dough, roll it out and use to line a shallow 10-in cake pan or deep pie pan. Spread the apricot jam over the base and sprinkle with the crushed cookies.

4 Slice the pears very thinly. Arrange the pear slices over the cookies in the pastry case. Sprinkle first with cinnamon then with raisins, and finally with the brown sugar.

5 Roll out a thin sausage shape using about ⅛ of the remaining dough, and place around the edge of the pie. Roll the remainder into thin sausages and arrange in a lattice over the pie, 4 or 5 strips in each direction, attaching to the strip around the edge.

6 Cook in a preheated oven for about 50 minutes until golden brown and cooked through. Remove from the oven and leave to cool. Serve warm or chilled, sprinkled with sifted confectioners' sugar.

STEP 3

STEP 4

STEP 5

CARAMELIZED ORANGE

The secret of these oranges is to allow them to marinate in the syrup for at least 24 hours, and preferably longer, so the caramel and liqueur can penetrate to the center of the fruit.

STEP 3

SERVES 6

6 large oranges
1 cup superfine sugar
1 cup water
6 whole cloves (optional)
2-4 tbsp Grand Marnier, Curaçao or brandy

1 Use a citrus zester or potato peeler to pare off the rind from 2 oranges, to give narrow strips of peel without any of the white pith attached. If using a potato peeler, cut the peel into very thin julienne strips using a very sharp knife.

2 Put the strips into a small saucepan and barely cover with water. Bring to the boil and simmer for 5 minutes until tender. Drain the strips and reserve the water.

3 Cut away all the white pith and peel from the oranges using a very sharp knife and then cut horizontally into 4 slices. Reassemble the oranges and hold in place with wooden toothpicks. Stand in a heatproof dish.

4 Put the sugar and water into a heavy-based saucepan with the cloves, if using. Bring to the boil and simmer gently until the sugar has

dissolved, then boil hard without stirring until the syrup thickens and begins to turn brown. Continue to cook until a light golden brown, then quickly remove from the heat and carefully pour in the reserved liquor from cooking the orange rind.

5 Return to a gentle heat until the caramel has fully dissolved again, then remove from the heat, add the liqueur or brandy. When mixed pour over the oranges.

6 Sprinkle the orange strips over the oranges, cover with plastic wrap and leave until cold. Chill for at least 3 hours and preferably for 24-48 hours before serving. If time allows, spoon the syrup over the oranges several times while they are marinating. Discard the toothpick before serving.

STEP 4

STEP 5

CARAMEL

To make caramel the sugar syrup is boiled until it turns golden brown and reaches the "small crack" stage, 280-305°F on a sugar thermometer.

STEP 6

STEP 1

STEP 2

STEP 4

STEP 5

RICOTTA ICE CREAM

*Ice cream is one of the traditional dishes of Italy. Everyone eats it and there are **gelato** stalls abounding which sell numerous flavors, usually in a cone. It is also served sliced, as in this classic from Sicily.*

SERVES 4-6

1/4 cup pistachio nuts
1/4 cup walnuts or pecan nuts
1/4 cup toasted chopped hazelnuts
grated rind of 1 orange
grated rind of 1 lemon
2 tbsp crystallized or stem ginger
2 tbsp glacé cherries
1/4 cup no-need-to-soak dried apricots
3 tbsp raisins
1 1/2 cups ricotta
2 tbsp Maraschino, Amaretto or brandy
1 tsp vanilla essence
4 egg yolks
1/2 cup superfine sugar

TO DECORATE:
whipped cream
few glacé cherries, pistachio nuts or mint
    leaves

1 Roughly chop the pistachio nuts and walnuts and mix with the toasted hazelnuts, orange and lemon rind. Finely chop the ginger, cherries, apricots, and raisins and add to the bowl.

2 Mix the ricotta evenly through the fruit mixture, then beat in the liqueur and vanilla essence.

3 Put the egg yolks and sugar in a bowl and whisk hard until very thick and creamy – they may be whisked over a saucepan of gently simmering water to speed up the process. Leave to cool, if necessary.

4 Carefully fold the ricotta mixture evenly through the beaten eggs and sugar until smooth.

5 Line a 7 x 5 in loaf pan with a double layer of plastic wrap or parchment paper, pour in the ricotta mixture, level the top, cover with more plastic wrap or parchment paper and chill in the freezer until firm – at least overnight.

6 To serve, carefully remove the ice cream from the pan and peel off the paper. Stand on a serving dish and if liked, decorate with whipped cream using a pastry bag and star nozzle, and glacé cherries and/or pistachio nuts. Serve in slices, with mint leaves.

ITALIAN FOOD BY REGION

generous 2¹/₂ cups all-purpose
flour
3 large eggs
1 tbsp olive oil
1 tbsp water
salt

1. To make the pasta dough, sift the flour and a pinch of salt onto a flat surface and make a well in the center.

2. Beat the eggs, oil and water together and gradually pour this liquid into the center of the flour, working in the flour with your hand, a little at a time until it all comes together to make a dough.

3. Knead for about 5 minutes until smooth. Cover with a damp cloth or put into a lightly oiled plastic bag and leave to rest for 5-15 minutes.

There are two main culinary zones in Italy: the wine and olive zone, which lies around Umbria, Liguria and the South; and the cattle country, where the olive tree will not flourish – Emilia-Romagna, Lombardy and Veneto – but where milk and butter are widely produced. Tuscany uses both butter and oil in its cooking because cattle flourish in the area and so do the olive trees.

PIEDMONT
The name means "at the foot of the mountain", which it is, bordering on both France and Switzerland. Its fertile arable fields are irrigated by the many canals which flow through the region.

The food is substantial, peasant-type fare, though the fragrant white truffle is found in this region. Truffles can be finely flaked or grated and added to many of the smarter dishes, but they are wildly expensive. There is also an abundance of wild mushrooms throughout the region. Garlic features strongly in the recipes and polenta, gnocchi and rice are eaten in larger quantities than pasta, the former offered as a first course when soup is not served. A large variety of game is also widely available in the area.

LOMBARDY
The mention of the capital, Milan, produces immediate thoughts of the wonderful risotto named after the city and also the Milanese soufflé flavored strongly with lemon. Veal dishes, including *vitello tonnato* and *osso buco*, are

specialites of the region, and other excellent meat dishes, particularly pot roasts, feature widely.

The lakes of the area produce a wealth of fresh fish. Rice and polenta are again popular but pasta also appears in many guises. The famous sweet yeasted cake Panettone is a product of this region.

TRENTINO-ALTO-ADIGE
This is a double area with a strong Germanic influence, particularly when it comes to the wines. There are also several liqueurs produced, still with a German influence, such as Aquavit, Kümmel and Slivovitz.

The foods are robust and basic in this mountainous area with rich green valleys and lakes where fish are plentiful. In the Trentino area, particularly, pasta and simple meat and variety meat dishes are popular, while in the Adige soups and pot roasts are favored, often with added dumplings and spiced sausages.

VENETO
The cooking in this northeast corner is straightforward, with abundant servings of polenta with almost everything. The land is intensely farmed, providing mostly cereals and wine. Pasta is more in the background with polenta, gnocchi and rice more favored. Fish, particularly seafood, is in abundance and especially good seafood salads are widely available. There are also excellent robust soups and risottos flavored with the seafood and sausages of the area.

LIGURIA

The Genoese are excellent cooks, and all along the Italian Riviera coast can be found fantastic trattoria which produce amazing fish dishes flavored with the local olive oil. Pesto sauce flavored with basil, cheese and pine nuts comes from this area, along with other excellent sauces. The aroma of fresh herbs abounds, widely used in many dishes, including their famous pizzas.

EMILIA-ROMAGNA

This is a special region of high gastronomic importance, with an abundance of everything, and rich food is widely served. Tortellini and lasagne feature widely, along with many other pasta dishes, as do saltimbocca and other veal dishes. Parma is famous for its ham, *prosciutto di Parma*, thought to be the best in the world. Balsamic vinegar, which has grown in popularity over the past decade, is also produced here, from wine which is distilled until it is dark brown and extremely strongly flavored.

TUSCANY

The Tuscans share a great pride in cooking and eating with the Emilians, and are known to have hefty appetites. Tuscany has everything: an excellent coastal area providing splendid fish, and hills covered in vineyards and fertile plains where every conceivable vegetable and fruit grows. There is plenty of game in the region, providing many interesting recipes; tripe cooked in a thick tomato sauce is popular along with many liver recipes; beans in many guises appear frequently, as well as pot roasts, steaks and full-bodied soups, all of which are well favored.

Florence has a wide variety of specialtes, while Siena boasts the famous candied fruit cake called Panforte di Siena.

UMBRIA/MARCHES

Inland Umbria is famous for its pork, and the character of the cuisine is marked by the use of the local fresh ingredients, including lamb, game and fish from the lakes, but is not spectacular on the whole. Spit-roasting and broiling is popular, and the excellent local olive oil is used both in cooking and to pour over dishes before serving. Black truffles, olives, fruit, and herbs are plentiful and feature in many recipes. Eastwards to the Marches the wealth of fish from the coast adds even more to the variety, and the food tends to be more on the elaborate side, with almost every restaurant noted for its excellent cuisine. First-class sausages and cured pork come from the Marches, particularly on the Umbrian border, and pasta features widely all over the region.

LAZIO

Rome is the capital of both Lazio and Italy and thus has become a focal point for specialites from all over Italy. Food from this region tends to be fairly simple and quick to prepare, hence the many pasta dishes with delicious sauces, gnocchi in various forms and plenty of dishes featuring lamb and veal (saltimbocca being just one), and variety meats, all with plenty of herbs and seasonings giving really robust flavors

COOKING PASTA

Pasta comes in all shapes and sizes and is available both fresh and dried. It is often said that the larger the pasta shapes, the richer the sauce should be, but that is a matter of preference: you can serve your favorite sauce with your favorite pasta, whatever the shape.

It is also said that guests should wait for the pasta to be ready and not vice versa; but, as pasta does not take long to cook, that should not present a problem. Always make sure it is served *al dente*, i.e., tender but still with a slight bite to it – soggy pasta is not very palatable, at least not to Italians and true lovers of pasta!

Allow 3-4 oz spaghetti or 1 cup short or small pasta per head for a main dish. Add to a saucepan of lightly salted gently simmering water, with a teaspoon of oil to help keep the pasta separate. Never fully cover the pot: either partly cover, or leave it totally uncovered, and once it has come back to the boil, give a good stir, reduce the heat and simmer for about 5 minutes for tiny pasta, 8-10 minutes for medium pasta and 10-15 minutes for large shapes. Fresh pasta of all types takes only a few minutes to cook. Always drain thoroughly before serving, and serve hot. For a salad, it may be rinsed under cold water to cool it down rapidly.

MAIN PASTA VARIETIES

Lasagne Everyone knows the flat pasta sheets, either plain or ridged, in plain egg, spinach and wholewheat varieties. Nowadays dried lasagne rarely needs pre-cooking, which speeds up the whole process. Simply layer with a fairly runny meat, fish or vegetable mixture together with a cheese or white sauce and brown in the oven.

Canneloni Large tubes which are usually stuffed with a meat, fish or vegetable mixture and cooked in a cheese sauce or strong garlic and tomato sauce. Canneloni can also be made by rolling up cooked sheets of lasagne around the filling.

Penne Shaped like quills with slanting ends and 1-1½ in long, they are always smooth tubes.

Tortellini Pasta pockets shaped into curls. Often filled with a meat, fish , cheese or vegetable forcemeat.

Spaghetti The best known type of pasta, available anywhere and everywhere.

Tagliatelle Narrow pasta strips, usually shaped into nests when sold dried. Available in egg, spinach, wholewheat and tomato flavors.

and delicious sauces. Vegetables feature along with the fantastic fruits, which are always in abundance in the local markets; and beans appear both in soups and many other dishes. The main theme of this region is strongly flavored food with robust sauces.

ABRUZZI AND MOLISE

Another divided region with an interior of mountains with river valleys, high plateaux, densely forested areas and a coastal plain. The cuisine here is deeply traditional, with local hams and cheeses from the mountain areas, interesting sausages with plenty of garlic and other seasonings, cured meats, wonderful fish and seafood, which is the main produce of the coastal areas, where fishing boats abound on the beaches. Lamb features widely: tender, juicy and well-flavored with herbs.

CAMPANIA

Naples is the home of pasta dishes, served with a splendid tomato sauce (with many variations) whose fame has spread worldwide. Pizza is said to have been created in Naples and now has spread to the north of the country and around the world.

Fish abounds, with *fritto misto* and *fritto pesce* being great favorites, varying daily depending on the catch. Fish stews are robust and varied, and shellfish in particular is often served with pasta. Cutlets and steaks are excellent, served with strong sauces usually flavored with garlic, tomatoes, and herbs: pizzaiola steak is one of the favorites. Excellent mozzarella cheese is produced locally and

used to create the crispy Mozarella in Carozza, again served with a garlicky tomato sauce. Sweet dishes are popular too, often with flaky pastry and ricotta cheese, and the seasonal fruit salads laced with wine or liqueur take a lot of beating.

PUGLIA (APULIA)

The ground is stony but it produces good fruit, olive groves, vegetables and herbs, and, of course, there is a large amount of seafood from the sea. Puglians are said to be champion pasta eaters: many of the excellent pasta dishes are exclusive to the region both in shape and ingredients. Mushrooms abound and are always added to the local pizzas.

Oysters and mussels are plentiful, and so is octopus. Brindisi is famous for its shellfish – both the seafood salads and risottos are truly memorable. But it is not all fish or pasta: lamb is roasted and stewed to perfection and so is veal, always with plenty of herbs.

BASILICATA

This is a sheep-farming area, mainly mountainous, where potent wines are produced to accompany a robust cuisine largely based on pasta, lamb, pork, game, and abundant dairy produce. The salamis and cured meats are excellent, as are the mountain hams. Lamb is flavored from the herbs and grasses on which it feeds. Wonderful thick soups – true minestrone – are produced in the mountains, and eels and fish are plentiful in the lakes. Chili peppers are grown in this region and appear in many of the recipes. They are not overpoweringly strong, although the flavors of the region in general tend to be quite strong and intense. The cheeses are excellent, with good fruits grown and interesting local bread baked in huge loaves.

CALABRIA

This is the toe of Italy, where orange and lemon groves flourish along with olive groves and a profusion of vegetables, especially eggplant, which are cooked in a variety of ways.

Chicken, rabbit, and guinea fowl are often on the menu. Pizzas feature largely, often with a fish topping. Mushrooms grow well in the Calabrian climate and feature in many dishes from sauces and stews to salads. Pasta comes with a great variety of sauces, including baby artichokes, eggs, meat, cheese, mixed vegetables, the large sweet bell peppers of the region, and of course, garlic. The fish is excellent too and here fresh tunafish and swordfish are available with many other varieties.

Like most southern Italians, the Calabrians are sweet-toothed and many desserts and cakes are flavored with aniseed, honey and almonds and feature the plentiful figs of the region.

SICILY

This is the largest island in the Mediterranean and the cuisine is largely based on fish and vegetables. Fish soups, stews and salads appear in unlimited forms, including tuna, swordfish, mussels, and many more; citrus fruits are widely grown along with almonds and pistachio nuts, and

the local wines, including marsala, are excellent.

Meat is often given a long, slow cooking, or else is ground and shaped before cooking. Game is plentiful and is often cooked in sweet-sour sauces containing the local black olives.

Pasta abounds again with more unusual sauces as well as the old favorites. All Sicilians have a love of desserts, cakes and especially ice cream. Cassata and other ice creams from Sicily are famous all over the world, and the huge variety of flavors of both cream ices and granita makes it difficult to decide which is your favorite.

SARDINIA

A pretty island with a wealth of flowers in the spring, but the landscape dries out in the summer from the hot sun. The national dish is suckling pig or newborn lamb cooked on an open fire or spit; and rabbit, game, and variety meat dishes are very popular.

The sweet dishes are numerous and often extremely delicate, and for non-sweet eaters there is fresh fruit of almost every kind in abundance.

Fish is top quality, with excellent sea bass, lobsters, tuna, mullet, eels and mussels in good supply.

The island has a haunting aroma which drifts from many kitchens – it is myrtle (*mirto*), a local herb that is added to anything and everything from chicken to the local liqueur; and along with the wonderful cakes and breads of Sardinia, myrtle will long remain a memory of the island when you have returned home.

Fettucine These are medium wide pasta strips with wavy edges, ideal to serve with meat and shellfish sauces.

Rigatoni Similar to penne but shorter and with a ridged surface.

Fusilli Also called spirals because they resemble corkscrews.They come in all colors and flavors including wholewheat, often mixed together. Also excellent in salads.

Farfalle These are bows of medium size, again made in all flavors of pasta to serve in a wide variety of hot dishes as well as salads.

Ravioli Square parcels of pasta with a spicy meat or cheese filling, cut with a shaped pasta cutter to give wavy edges, then poached and served in a variety of sauces.

Macaroni A fairly thick, tubular pasta available in different lengths and thicknesses. Some are almost straight while others are curved, and called "elbow" macaroni. Ideal to serve with any type of sauce and also great in salad.

INDEX

Abruzzi and Molise, 78
almonds: Panforte di Siena, 68
anchovies: Crostini alla Fiorentina, 18
   Vitello Tonnato, 52
antipasto, 7, 14-21
apricots: Panforte di Siena, 68
   ricotta ice cream, 74
Apulia, 78

Basil: pesto, 13
Basilicata, 78-9
beans: red bean soup, 10
beef: pizzaiola steak, 51
   Sicilian spaghetti, 27
bread: crostini, 18
   Mozzarella in carozza, 17

Cakes: Panforte di Siena, 68
Calabria, 79
Calabrian pizza, 36
Campania, 78
canneloni, 78
caramelized oranges, 73
casserole, squid, 46
cheese: Calabrian pizza, 36
   gnocchi Romana, 29
   Mozzarella in carozza, 17
   pesto, 13
cherries (glacé): ricotta ice cream, 74
chicken: chicken with green olives, 59
   tortellini, 24
clams: seafood salad, 21
coffee: tiramisu, 64
cream cheese: ricotta ice cream, 74
   tiramisu, 64
Crostini alla Fiorentina, 18

Desserts, 63-74

Eggplant:
   eggplant salad, 14
   Sicilian spaghetti, 27
eggs: zabaglione, 67
Emilia-Romagna, 77

Farfalle, 79
fish, 39-46
   baked red snapper, 40
   fish soup, 8
   sardine and potato bake, 42
   squid casserole, 46
   trout in red wine, 44
fusilli, 79

Garlic: baked red snapper, 40

garlic mayonnaise, 21
ginger: ricotta ice cream, 74
gnocchi Romana, 29
Grand Marnier: caramelized
   oranges, 73

Hake: seafood salad, 21
ham: Mozzarella in carozza, 17
   saltimbocca, 56
   tagliatelle with pumpkin, 32
   tortellini, 24
hazelnuts: Panforte di Siena, 68
   ricotta ice cream, 74
honey: Panforte di Siena, 68

Ice cream, ricotta, 74

Lamb, pot roast leg of, 54
lasagne, 78
Lazio, 77-8
Liguria, 77
liver: Crostini alla Fiorentina, 18
   liver with wine sauce, 61
Lombardy, 76

Macaroni, 79
Marches, 77
Marsala: zabaglione, 67
mascarpone: tiramisu, 64
mayonnaise, garlic, 21
meat and poultry, 49-61
Milanese risotto, 34
minestrone with pesto, 13
monkfish: seafood salad, 21
Mozzarella in carozza, 17
mushrooms: chicken with
   green olives, 59
   polenta, 31
   tortellini, 24
mussels: fish soup, 8
   seafood salad, 21

Olives: chicken with green olives, 59
orange, caramelized, 73

Panforte di Siena, 68
pasta, 23
   cooking, 77
   pasta dough, 76
   Sicilian spaghetti, 27
   tagliatelle with pumpkin, 32
   tortellini, 24
   varieties, 78-9
pâtés: Crostini alla Fiorentina, 18
pear tart, 71

penne, 78
peppers bell: Calabrian pizza, 36
   chicken with green olives, 59
   squid casserole, 46
   tomato and pepper sauce, 17
pesto, minestrone with, 13
Piedmont, 76
pine nuts: pesto, 13
pistachio nuts: ricotta ice cream, 74
pizza, Calabrian, 36
pizzaiola steak, 51
polenta, 31
potatoes: sardine and potato bake, 42
poultry and meat, 49-61
prosciutto: Mozzarella in carozza, 17
   Saltimbocca, 56
   tagliatelle with pumpkin, 32
   tortellini, 24
Puglia, 78
pumpkin, tagliatelle with, 32

Ravioli, 79
red kidney beans: red bean soup, 10
red snapper, baked, 40
rice: Milanese risotto, 34
ricotta ice cream, 74
rigatoni, 79
risotto, Milanese, 34

Saffron: Milanese risotto, 34
salads: eggplant, 14
   seafood, 21
salami: Calabrian pizza, 36
Saltimbocca, 56
sardine and potato bake, 42
Sardinia, 79
sauces: garlic, 40
   mushroom, 31
   tomato and pepper, 17
seafood salad, 21
semolina: gnocchi Romana, 29
shellfish and fish, 39-46
shrimp: fish soup, 8
   seafood salad, 21
Sicilian spaghetti, 27
Sicily, 79
soups, 7-13
   fish, 8
   minestrone with pesto, 13
   red bean, 10
spaghetti, 78
   Sicilian spaghetti, 27
spinach: tortellini, 24
squid: preparation, 46
   seafood salad, 21

squid casserole, 46

Tagliatelle, 78
   tagliatelle with pumpkin, 32
tart, pear, 71
tiramisu, 64
tomatoes: Calabrian pizza, 36
   fish soup, 8
   pizzaiola steak, 51
   pot roast leg of lamb, 54
   sardine and potato bake, 42
   Sicilian spaghetti, 27
   squid casserole, 46
   tomato and pepper sauce, 17
tortellini, 24, 78
Trentino-Alto-Adige, 76
trout in red wine, 44
tuna: Vitello Tonnato, 52
Tuscany, 77

Umbria, 77

Veal: Saltimbocca, 56
   Vitello Tonnato, 52
vegetables: minestrone with pesto, 13
Veneto, 76
Vitello Tonnato, 52

Walnuts: ricotta ice cream, 74
wine: liver with wine sauce, 61
   trout in red wine, 44

Zabaglione, 67